# I Got a Job
## and it wasn't that bad

**by Jim**

D0111518

**Andrews and McMeel**
A Universal Press Syndicate Company
**Kansas City**

*Jim's Journal* daily cartoon strip is syndicated by Onion Features Syndicate.

*I Got a Job and it wasn't that bad* copyright © 1993 by Dikkers. All rights reserved. Printed in the United States of America. No part of this book may be used or reproduced in any manner whatsoever without written permission except in the case of reprints in the context of reviews. For information write Andrews and McMeel, a Universal Press Syndicate Company, 4900 Main Street, Kansas City, Missouri 64112.

ISBN: 0-8362-1709-8

Library of Congress Catalog Card Number: 92-74806

I went out looking for a job today.

Tony said I should stuff envelopes on my own time at home. "That's what I'm doing!" he said.

I went to a movie theater and the manager said they didn't need anybody.

But he gave me an application anyway and said he'd put it on file.

Yesterday I applied for jobs at a copy shop, a book store, a clothing store, a futon store, a movie theater, a newspaper and a bank.

Today I took all the applications back.

Most people said they'd call me and let me know.

It didn't seem like anybody would hire me, but I'm sure I'll get a job somewhere.

I bought a news-paper today.

I read it while I ate some toasted bagels.

When I finished eating, I sat there for a while and read some more.

Tony walked by, flipped through the paper and took the sports section and entertainment section.

Today I was sitting at my desk, reading.

Every once in a while Mr. Peterson would run by my door really fast, playing.

Once he stopped right in front of it and looked at me with his eyes wide open.

Then he took off running as fast as he could.

Tony flipped his calendar to March yesterday.

It's the Sports Illustrated swimsuit calendar. He got it for Christmas.

"I love it," he said today. "But I get sick of seeing the same girl all month."

"If they had a different girl for every day," he said, "that'd be something."

Today I was just sitting around watching TV. (Bewitched was on.)

Kurt, Tony's friend, came over. He was eating a bag of cheese puffs.

Tony wasn't around, so Kurt came in and waited for him.

He sat and watched Bewitched with me and laughed out loud.

Today Tony said we needed a shelf for our apartment.

So he, Steve and I drove to a furniture store and bought one.

Tony tied the trunk on top of it and said, "That ain't goin' nowhere!"

When we first got it home Tony couldn't find a place for it.

Steve got the mail today.

He walked up to me, flipping through the letters.

"Nothing for you, Jim," he said.

"I guess nobody likes you," he said.

I found a dime on the sidewalk today.

Even though a dime isn't worth much, I felt pretty good about finding it.

After walking a ways farther, I almost thought I saw another dime.

But it was just a little round metal thing.

Ruth stopped by to visit me today.

We got talking about when we used to work at McDonald's.

We laughed pretty hard, remembering the good times and the funny things we did.

Ruth tried to stop laughing and delicately cleared her throat.

I was sitting at my desk today trying to read.

But I didn't really feel like reading.

I accidentally flicked a tiny piece of notebook paper fringe on the floor and Mr. Peterson jumped on it.

I flicked more fringes and Mr. Peterson jumped on all of them.

Today I was sitting around nibbling on some potato chips.

Steve was making himself some lunch and singing "Tutti-frutti."

The whole apartment was pretty quiet except for Steve's slightly out-of-tune singing.

After a few minutes, Tony yelled from the other room, "Will you shut up!"

Yesterday I was thirsty for some orange juice, so I went to the store to buy some.

I looked at all the tabloids while I waited in line.

Today Steve said, "Hey, Jim, can I have some of your orange juice?"

I said yes.

Then Tony came by and said, "Hey-OJ! Can I have some?"

I said yes.

I got a call from the bookstore today.

(I applied for a job there the other day.)

I'm supposed to go in for an interview tomorrow.

I felt pretty good about it, but Tony says jobs are for proles.

I went to the bookstore today to interview for a job.

BOOKS

OPEN

I talked to Jean, the manager, who had a bunch of keys hanging from her belt.

She told me about the job and said I could start tomorrow if I was interested.

Then she asked me where I was from and that kind of thing.

I told Steve and Tony I got a job at the bookstore.

"That's fantastic!" Tony said. "You can buy books for us with the company discount!"

He made a list of all the books he wanted.

Steve said he was planning to get the Cliffs Notes for Great Expectations and asked if we had it in stock.

I said I didn't know.

Today was my first day on the job at the bookstore.

A guy named Paul taught me shipping and receiving.

"You find the packing slip, then you fill out one of these forms and file it under the publisher."

That was all he said.

I wasn't really sure what I was supposed to do.

Last night I was washing my face in the sink.

When I was done I didn't feel like moving or drying my face off.

I just let the water drip off my face for a while.

I went to work at the bookstore today.

Nobody ever really explained what I was supposed to do when I started shipping & receiving the other day.

Jean, the manager, seems pretty nice, so I asked her what I was supposed to be doing.

"Shipping and receiving!" she said.

I got up a little late today.

I wanted a bowl of cereal but we were out of milk.

I went to the corner store to buy some more.

When I came back I ate my bowl of cereal and gave Mr. Peterson some milk too.

Today Tony was watching Jeopardy and eating some hot dogs.

Mr. Peterson was standing on his hind legs in front of Tony.

He put some ketchup on his finger and Mr. Peterson licked it off.

"Hey," Tony yelled, "Mr. Peterson likes ketchup. I can't believe this crazy cat."

When my alarm went off this morning I didn't feel like getting up at all.

I laid in bed while my clock-radio played Your Kiss Is on My List, by Hall and Oates.

I was too lazy to get up and turn it off.

That song stuck in my head for the whole day.

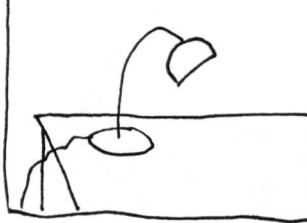

The bulb in my lamp burned out today so I bought a new one.

I went to the hardware store.

I found the bulb, brought it to the register, and the man said, "So, will this be all for you today?"

I said yes, and he rang it up.

beep beep

Today I was just sitting around in my room.

Tony came in and said, "Hey, what's the word for being innocent in a trial?"

"Why can't I think of it? It's right on the tip of my tongue," he said.

I couldn't think of it either.

We couldn't believe neither of us could think of it. Finally I realized it was acquitted.

At the bookstore today I started getting the hang of shipping and receiving.

Paul, the guy who trained me, was there.

He didn't say much. He looked kind of tired.

Once he grunted and said, "This is a hell hole."

Today I was just sitting around watching TV

A really old movie was on. Cary Grant was in it.

Tony watched it for a while too.

We laughed at some parts of it.

Tony asked me how I liked working at the bookstore and I said it was okay.

Today at the bookstore Jean came down to shipping & receiving, where I work.

I asked her why Paul is always so grumpy.

She said Paul is only like that when he's down here.

She said after a while I'll get to work upstairs and I'll realize how rotten shipping and receiving is.

Today Tony and I were watching TV when it broke all of a sudden.

The sound was still there, but the picture was completely fuzzy.

Tony tried to fix it, but he couldn't.

He hit the side of it then looked at it for a few seconds. "That usually works," he said.

Today I went to the store to buy some cottage cheese and a pear.

On my way home I saw the newspaper in one of those dispensers.

It looked like it might be kind of interesting, so I bought one.

I went home and ate my pear and cottage cheese and read the newspaper.

Today at the bookstore we unloaded boxes of books from a delivery truck.

Jean looked inside and noticed that the books weren't the ones she ordered.

She was angry, and talked to the driver, then called the distributor.

I took the long way home from work.

It was a pleasant walk.

| | | | |
|---|---|---|---|
| Today Steve rented Robocop and we all watched it.  | It was pretty good.  | Afterwards, I made myself a tuna sandwich.  | Mr. Peterson kept jumping up on the counter even though I kept setting him back on the floor.  |
| I had a hard time getting up today.  | My alarm went off at 7, but I reset it for 7:30.  | At 7:30 I reset it for 8, and at 8 I reset it for 8:30.  | I thought I'd feel more like getting up each time, but I never did.  |

**Today I was just sitting around when the phone rang.**

**It was somebody who wanted to ask me some questions for a marketing survey.**

**I answered her questions even though they didn't seem very important.**

**When she was done she thanked me as if I'd done a great deed.**

**Today Steve said he's going to some friends' house to watch videos tonight.**

**"They rented all the 'Halloween' sequals. Wanna come?"**

**I said I'd rather stay home.**

**Tony and his friends planned a night out too.**

**One of his friends was wearing a Pat Sajak mask.**

**They said they'd raise some hell tonight.**

This morning I was eating a bowl of cereal.

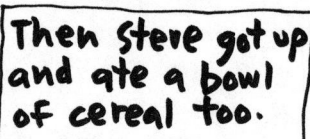

Then Steve got up and ate a bowl of cereal too.

Then Tony sat down and ate sweet tarts and tootsie rolls.

"I got these last night," he said. "We went out trick-or-treating and actually got some candy!"

At work today I stocked shelves.

Jean taught me how to do it the other day.

I feel like I'm getting to know this job better.

Once, somebody asked me where the history section was—and I knew.

**Panel 1:** Today I was walking down the sidewalk.

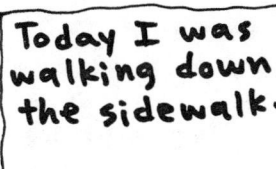

**Panel 2:** An ambulance drove by and its siren was so loud it hurt my ears.

**Panel 3:** Then I started thinking how strange the cracks in the sidewalk would be if you were really small.

**Panel 4:** They'd be like giant trenches with rocks and other residue collected in there.

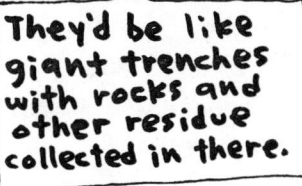

**Panel 5:** Today I was taking out the garbage to the dumpster behind our building.

**Panel 6:** Tony came running after me saying, "Jim, wait! Don't throw that away!"

**Panel 7:** He rummaged through the bag.

**Panel 8:** "Ah ha! There it is!" he said, holding up half a piece of paper with some writing on it.

Today Steve asked Tony and me if we wanted a part in a movie.

He has to make one for a film class he's taking.

Tony said, "Why not? I think I could act pretty good."

Steve told Tony he'd have to act like a real jerk for the part he had in mind.

Steve started filming his movie today.

I helped.

We filmed on the sidewalk just outside our apartment building.

Tony had to walk down the sidewalk and throw litter in the grass.

Steve had him do it two or three times and Tony said, "This is boring. C'mon, let's get moving."

| | | | |
|---|---|---|---|
| Today Tony asked Steve what his movie was going to be about.  | Steve said it was going to be kind of experi-mental.  | Tony said, "It's not gonna suck is it?"  | Steve said, "I hope not," and chuckled.  |
| Steve finished filming his movie today.  | Tony had to kill himself with a piece of glass.  | Steve wanted to put ketchup all over Tony's shirt.  | They got into a big argument because Tony wanted to put on a different shirt and Steve said he couldn't because it wouldn't make any sense in the movie. |

We were all just sitting around watching TV today.

Mr. Peterson ran past us as fast as he could.

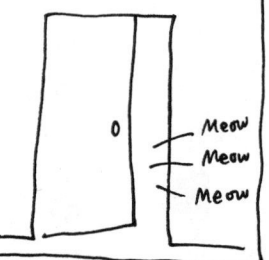
He went into another room and meowed over and over.

Meow
Meow
Meow

We went in there and couldn't figure out what all the fuss was about— he was just sitting there.

Today Steve showed Tony and me the movie he made.

It was fun to see all the shots we filmed all put together. And he had music for it too— the Peter Gunn theme.

Tony kept saying, "This isn't bad, I'm a pretty good actor."

Steve told us he got a C and we couldn't believe it.

I bought a book today – Anthem, by Ayn Rand.

I decided I needed something to read.

It's really short, so it shouldn't take me too long to read, I figured.

I meant to read a little bit before I went to sleep, but I stayed up till 3 a.m. and read the whole thing.

Steve came home today eating some of that long stick candy that you lick and dip into flavored powder.

"I haven't had this stuff since I was a kid," he said.

Tony said, "How can you even think of eating that crap?"

"It's just sugar is all it is!" he said.

Today when I got up Tony was watching CNN News.

He told me he wanted to keep up with current events more.

"It's important to know what's going on in the world," he said.

At work today I put little magazine subscription flyers inside new books.

I've been learning to run the cash register at the bookstore.

It was pretty busy today.

I told one guy that his text books would cost $140.

He got out his checkbook and said, "If money is all you love, then that's what you'll receive."

Today I walked by a newspaper recycling bin and noticed a plastic cup in it.

I thought to my self that the cup shouldn't be in there.

But I didn't take it out and throw it in the trash can.

I figured somebody else would probably sort it out eventually.

Last night Tony said he was going to a big party.

"Don't wait up for me!" he told Steve and me.

He came home late, drinking a beer. "This is only my third," he said, "and it hasn't even affected me."

"It's like the situation in China," he said.

Then he made an analogy between the two things in a babbling sort of way.

Today while I was taking a shower the water suddenly scalded me twice.

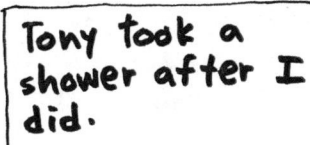

Tony took a shower after I did.

After he was in there a while he suddenly yelled, "Ouch! Geez, what's going on here?"

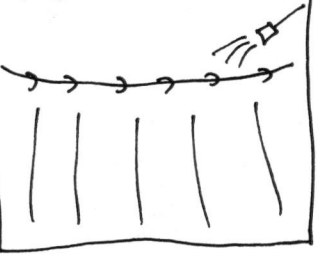

About a minute later he yelled, "Aaaah!! Damn this water!"

Today Tony and I were sitting around watching TV.

Tony was flipping around the channels with the remote control.

Steve came up and said we should ask our landlord to fix our scalding shower.

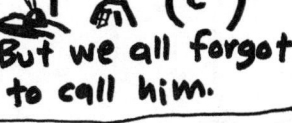

Tony said, "Yeah, I'll give that bum a piece of my mind." But we all forgot to call him.

| | | | |
|---|---|---|---|
| Today Tony visited the people who live next door to us.  | He figured out that our shower turns scalding hot whenever they flush their toilet.  | He called our landlord and told him to fix it.  | When he hung up, he said, "It's as easy as that. He said he'd fix it tomorrow."  |
| While Tony was taking a shower this morning, he swore like crazy, over and over.  | Steve and I avoided him for a while afterwards.  | He called our landlord and said, "Hey, would you fix our shower? You said you'd fix it last week!"  | When he hung up, he said, "What a bum."  |

Today a maintenance man from the landlord's company fixed our shower.

(It was scalding us whenever the neighbors flushed their toilet.)

Mr. Peterson sniffed the man's shoes while he was working, then ran away whenever the man moved.

When the man was done, he said, "That oughta do it for ya."

Today Rick and I were loading books into upstairs storage.

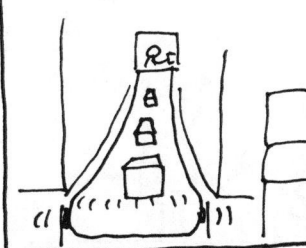

We had fun riding up the conveyor belt and making jokes.

He told me he had a crush on his roommate.

I don't know why he told me. It didn't really fit in the conversation.

I guess he just needed to tell somebody.

Steve got the mail today.

He gave me mine and said, "Hey, Jim, you may have already won two million dollars."

Then Steve and Tony made fun of me, thinking of how I'd spend two million dollars.

I watched the crumbs of my peanut butter and jelly sandwich fall onto my plate.

Today I got up early and was really tired.

I got out of bed thinking I might be able to wake up.

But I was too tired, so I decided to go back to sleep.

But Mr. Peterson was lying on my pillow.

At the bookstore for the past few weeks Jean's had us reorganizing downstairs storage.

Rick and I were supposed to be down there today sorting stuff.

But we hardly did any work, and mostly just talked and joked around.

And Jean was too busy running the store upstairs, so she never checked up on us.

Today Ruth, Steve and I went to eat at Wendy's.

Steve was telling us how much he couldn't wait to get out of school.

"I loved school," Ruth said. "I wish I could go back."

Steve couldn't believe Ruth liked school, and said, "You can take my place then."

I was watching TV and eating a hot dog today when the phone rang.

Tony answered it and said, "Jim's busy watching Green Acres, can I take a message?"

But he was just kidding, and handed me the phone.

It was Jean, from the bookstore. She wanted to know if I could work Saturdays.

I told her I could.

Today at the bookstore Rick and I had to price 25 boxes of new books and put them on the shelf.

We figured out the price from the invoice, which we're supposed to do, then put stickers on.

But Jean saw the books and said the prices were wrong. We used wholesale instead of retail prices.

We had to peel off all the stickers and put new ones on.

Today Tony and I were watching TV.

The NBC Nightly News was on.

"I'm gonna get so sloshed tonight," Tony said.

At the bookstore today I was shelving self-help books.

There was dust and crumpled-up gum wrappers way back behind the books.

Rick, who was working with me, walked by and said, "Those shelves could use some dusting, but don't tell Jean!"

I decided Rick was probably right.

I went to the grocery store today.

I wanted to buy some oranges. But they had a bad selection.

They all had bruised or molded spots, and were displayed so you couldn't see the spots.

But I managed to find a couple good oranges.

At the bookstore today I was punching in on the time clock.

I noticed Jean laughing and trying to run away from Rick.

Jean had a secret about Rick and was going to tell everybody.

I didn't know what it was all about, but everybody was having a good time—even Rick.

| | | | |
|---|---|---|---|
| Today Steve said he was going to get Mr. Peterson fixed.  | "That's mean," Tony said. "You should let him sow his wild oats first."  | Steve told Tony that everybody he talked to said it's best to fix cats early.  | I looked at Mr. Peterson and it almost seemed like he knew his fate was being discussed.  |
| Steve took Mr. Peterson to the vet today to get neutered.  | Mr. Peterson has been to the vet before, and doesn't like it.  | When Steve came back he said, "Hey, guess what. Mr. Peterson's a girl." | Tony was watching TV, and he mumbled, "Big deal, a cat's a cat."  |

Today Steve brought Mr. Peterson back from the vet.

She had a little square bald spot on her stomach, and looked tired.

Today at the bookstore I worked the cash register.

Jean, the manager, came up to me and said, "How's it goin', Jim?"

I said I was fine, and told her about Mr. Peterson getting fixed.

She said, "You remind me of my little brother."

When I came home from work today Mr. Peterson was sitting on the couch.

She looked at me while I came in and took off my coat.

I sat next to her for a while and scratched her head, but she didn't purr like usual.

Then I got up and made a tuna sandwich.

I worked at the bookstore again today.

Somebody was sick and Jean called me in to work.

I was doing invoicing when Jean came up to me.

"The shelves in the self-help section are filthy," she said. "Jim, why don't you dust those shelves when you're done here."

I got up around 8:30 today.

I noticed Tony sleeping in his clothes on the couch.

I took a shower, poured a bowl of cereal, and a lot of other noisy things.

And Tony didn't wake up— he didn't even turn over.

I did a load of laundry today.

I got the washing machine started and went back to my room.

When I came back, the clothes were all covered with grains of soap, even though the machine was done.

I figured that machine was broken. So I washed my clothes in a different one and they came out fine.

Today I worked on the cash register at the bookstore.

Hardly any people came in to buy anything.

So I just sat there and didn't have to work very hard.

Today I was sitting around petting Mr. Peterson.

I scratched up and down her back and she purred like crazy then fell asleep on my lap.

After a few minutes, the phone rang, so I had to get up and answer it.

I lifted her up and set her down on the chair, and she stayed in the exact same position she was in on my lap.

Today I took a walk around town.

I went to an art gallery and looked at the art.

It was nice to get away from everything for a while.

| | | | |
|---|---|---|---|
| Today when I got up I was really tired. | I set my alarm for an hour later and went back to sleep. | When I got up again, I was still really tired. | When I got up and saw Steve, he said, "Rise and shine, Jim!" and that made me feel like going back to sleep again. |
|  | 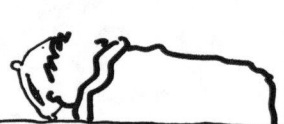 |  |  |

| | | | |
|---|---|---|---|
| Today Tony was listening to a top-40 radio station. | He was cleaning up some of his stuff around the apartment, singing along with the music. | Then some commercials came on—the kind with music in them. | And Tony sang along with those too. |
| 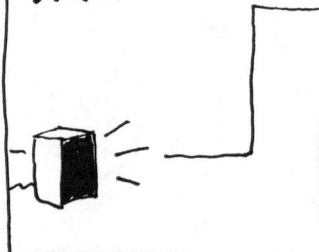 |  |  |  |

Today I was reading a book at the cash register at the bookstore.

Jean told me to put the book away so I could watch what I was doing.

But nobody was in the store, so there was nothing to watch.

Today I bumped into Dean, a guy I sort of knew in college.

We talked for just a couple minutes about school, and he joked about his coat, which he got for Christmas.

We came to a corner and he said, "I go this way, see you around, Jim."

I walked aways more and for a brief second I couldn't remember who I'd bumped into.

I was in the kitchen washing dishes today while Tony was eating a pot pie.

Once, he looked up like he was deep in thought.

He said, "I've decided something: paper towels are a complete waste."

"Why waste money on paper towels when you can wash a real towel as much as you want and use it over and over?" he said.

Today at the bookstore Jean said, "Jim, would you come see me when your shift's over with?"... I worked for $5\frac{1}{2}$ hours and that whole time tried to imagine what she might have to say.

When I finally talked to her, she said she had to let some people go, and since I didn't have seniority, I'd be one of them.

She said she was sorry and wished she didn't have to do it.

While I walked home, the traffic, people, and all the other noises seemed a lot more vivid than usual.

Last night I was bored, so I turned on the radio and flipped around the stations.

I found some relaxing music and just sat there and listened to it for a long time.

I called to make an appointment with a dentist today.

They said they had an opening tomorrow.

Also today I sat outside for a while and looked at the sidewalk.

I had my dentist appointment today.

I sat in the waiting room for a few minutes and read People magazine.

The dentist used rubber gloves when he cleaned and checked my teeth, and I could taste and smell the rubber.

My teeth felt smooth and clean when I left.

Today I noticed Mr. Peterson clawing up the stereo speakers.

scratch scratch scratch

Tony saw her too, and said, "Shoo! Shoo! Those are expensive speakers, you goofy little varmint!"

Steve told Tony that the speaker covers are only decorative, and clawing didn't damage the speakers at all.

"Maybe you'd feel different if they were _your_ speakers," Tony said.

(They're Tony's.)

I took Mr. Peterson outside today.

We just sat on the steps outside our building.

Mr. Peterson was really tense and darted her head around at every little sound.

When I tried to take her back inside, she sniffed my hand like she didn't know who I was.

Today Steve bought a leash for Mr. Peterson so he can take her outside.

"It's spring after all," Steve said.

He put the leash on her and she flipped around trying to get it off.

Tony and Steve laughed like crazy.

When I got out of the shower this morning I realized my towel wasn't there.

I thought I might have left it in my room because I was going to do some laundry.

I used Tony's towel to dry myself off.

It smelled like Tony.

Steve and Ruth and I rented a movie last night and ate popcorn out of a big bowl.

Mr. Peterson kept sitting up to look inside the bowl.

"Look out Mr. Peterson, you'll tip over the bowl," Ruth kept saying.

Mr. Peterson kept sitting up to look, but never tipped over the bowl.

Today I was walking into our apt. building when I saw Tony sunbathing in the lawn.

He was playing some rap music on his radio.

"You ought to come out here, man, the sun is great," he said.

When I said I didn't feel like it, he said, "I swear you'd make a great hermit, Jim."

Last night I wasn't tired enough to get to sleep.

I sat in bed and let my mind wander.

I got thinking about being locked in a dungeon in a castle and how I'd escape.

I don't know what I thought about after that. I must have fallen asleep.

I moved into my own apartment today.

(Steve, Tony and I decided to get different apartments a few months ago.)

(Tony is living in the same building as me only down the hall.)

My new place is really small.

I was sitting in the kitchen today eating a sandwich.

Mr. Peterson was sitting by the door, meowing.

I let her out in the hall for a while.

After she got over being scared of it, she ran up and down the hall really fast.

I watched a street juggler today for a while.

when he was done he juggled five balls and flipped his hat out for a finish.

Then he asked everybody to put money in the hat.

Most people walked away. He looked right at me and I felt guilty so I gave him some money.

I saw Tony today.

He'd just gotten his mail.

He was pretty happy about something. He said, "Hey ho, Jim."

He shook an envelope in my face and laughed, "He he he hee!"

"It had a big check in it," he said.

Today I went to the library and checked out a book.

It was Cider House Rules. I figured it'd be a pretty good book to read.

When I was walking into my apartment, a guy said. "How are you today?"

I told him I was fine.

Ruth and I rented an old black-and-white Flash Gordon movie today.

Ruth said she normally doesn't care for science fiction, but thought this was pretty good.

**Today I slept in really late because I didn't feel like getting up.**

**Mr. Peterson was sleeping on the floor in a spot where the sun was shining through.**

**I wanted to eat something but I didn't have enough energy to make anything.**

**Then I watched TV.**

**My mom called today.**

**She said she was going on a trip to San Francisco**

**(for a piano-teaching conference).**

**She said she was really excited about going and said she'd send me a post card.**

Today I called Steve to see if he wanted to do something.

He came over and we just sat around.

His tennis shoes were stark white.

I asked him if he got new shoes and he said yes.

I've been reading Cider House Rules. It's a pretty good book.

Today when I was reading it, Mr. Peterson jumped up on my lap.

She sat right on the book, so I couldn't read it.

Today I walked by a movie theater.

It was the early afternoon, so they were closed.

I looked inside and it was completely dark.

I looked at the movie poster outside—it had creases in it from being folded.

Today when I was opening the door to my apartment, I saw this guy from a few doors down.

He was walking very briskly.

"Hey, how's it goin'?" he said.

I told him everything was going fine.

**Today I was walking around outside.**

**I was waiting to cross a busy street when I noticed a particular car go by.**

**It had a bunch of people in it waving wildly at me.**

**But I didn't recognize them or anything.**

**Today I was tired so I took a nap. It was around 3 p.m.**

**When I got up it was dark outside.**

**I couldn't believe I slept so long.**

**I watched TV and noticed everything was running late.**

**It was because of a presidential address or something.**

Today my phone rang and I answered it.

Nobody was there, so I hung up.

It rang again, and nobody was there again, so I hung up.

The third time it started ringing I just let it ring, and it rang a million times.

Steve and I were sitting around watching TV today.

There was a commercial on for a car or something.

Steve said, "Yeah, right," in response to one of the claims the ad made.

"Commercials are just the dumbest things," he said.

I went to a park today, sat on a bench and tossed popcorn to the ducks.

It was fun watching them.

One duck was afraid of the popcorn and wouldn't go near it.

Another duck loved the popcorn. He was really small, but would challenge ducks twice his size to get at each kernel.

Today Ruth told me she was going to visit her parents for a few days.

"I really miss seeing my family," she said.

Then she said, "Jim, you should come with me! It would be really fun!"

So I said I would.

**Panel 1:** I stopped by Tony's apartment today.

**Panel 2:** He asked me how everything was going and offered me a can of soda.

**Panel 3:** The soda company had an instant-win game on the can.

Be an Instant Winner! $ $ $ $

**Panel 4:** Tony said if my can turned out to be a winner, he'd get to claim the money because he bought the soda.

**Panel 5:** I went out for a walk today.

**Panel 6:** I walked quite a ways, but never got tired or felt like stopping.

**Panel 7:** It seemed like the more I walked, the more invigorated I got

**Panel 8:** I bet I walked for three hours.

Today Steve brought a couple of friends over.

One of them saw Mr. Peterson and said, "oh, look, a kitty! She's so cute!"

They stayed around a few minutes, then left.

After they left, Mr. Peterson sat by the door like she wanted to go out too.

Today Ruth picked me up to go to her parents' house

(She invited me to come along with her the other day.)

She said, "I really like this little car," but kept talking about things like the radio not sounding very good and the gas gauge not working.

We drove for almost five hours.

Last night Ruth and I arrived at her parents' house.

Ruth's mom met us at the door and said, "Is this the friend you brought along?"

Ruth's parents started asking us how our trip was, and Ruth's dad was mostly watching the news on TV.

Today Ruth and her mom made everybody breakfast. Ruth's sister was telling me she could play the clarinet.

Today Ruth and I left her parents' house.

Ruth's mom said, "It was fun having you, Jim. Come back and visit any time."

Once we got on the road, Ruth talked about her family and her dog.

She also said she picked up some tapes from her house so we could listen to them in the car.

Today I did some laundry.

I walked down to the basement where the washing machines are.

In the stairway I passed the guy who lives down the hall from me.

"Doin' some laundry?" he said.

I watched a game show today.

Contestants had to guess the meanings of made-up personalized license plates.

I also finished reading Cider House Rules today.

It was a pretty good book.

Today I went to a diner.

I ate an order of fries and read a newspaper.

The diner had a lot of odd things hanging on the wall.

DIKKERS

There was a giant airplane propeller and also a page from a children's book that they framed.

Today when I got up my throat was sore—it felt like it was closed up.

When I talked, it sounded like I was squawking.

Tony said, "What's the matter, Jim? You entering puberty?"

My throat got less sore as the day wore on.

I stayed home today and wrapped myself in a blanket and watched TV.

I hardly ever got hungry, and when I did I only ate soup.

There are some really dumb TV shows on in the day time.

I stood and stared in the mirror today.

I got really close and looked at the tiny patterns in the iris part of my eye.

Mr. Peterson was walking around the sink, which is right under the mirror.

I lifted her up to show her herself in the mirror, but she didn't seem to be interested in it.

Steve and I were walking by a copy store today.

There was a "help wanted" sign in the window, and Steve said he should apply.

We went in to get an application and I decided to fill one out, too.

I wrote down my experience at McDonald's and the book store, but couldn't remember the exact dates I worked there.

I got a postcard from my mom today.

It was from San Francisco, where she went for a piano teachers conference.

She said she was having a great time riding trolleys, seeing the Golden Gate Bridge and stuff.

I couldn't read it in the top right-hand corner because the postmark covered up her writing.

Today Tony told me he needed to write a resumé.

He showed me a book he bought on how to write a resumé.

The Complete Resumé Handbook

He also got resumés from some friends to use as guides.

"I'm ready to go!" he said.

Then he asked me if I knew how to write a resumé.

Tony bought a new tape today, and he was listening to it while he worked on his resumé.

(It was a Fine Young Cannibals tape.)

| | | | |
|---|---|---|---|
| Today I got a call from the manager of the copy store.  | He said he wanted me to come down for an interview.  | (I applied for a job there the other day with Steve.)  | I went there and met the manager. His name was Hal.  |
| Today I told Steve I got a job at the copy store.  | He said it was no fair that we both applied and only I got the job.  | Then Tony said, "Steve, why would you even want a peon job like that? You need to start thinking <u>management</u>."  | "My brother," Tony said, "is manager of a shoe store and makes more money than all of us!"  |

**Panel 1:** I was sitting around today not doing much of anything when I heard somebody pounding on my window.

**Panel 2:** It was Tony, and I heard him yell through the glass, "Could you let me in the building—I lost my keys!"

**Panel 3:** I went out and opened the door for him.

**Panel 4:** "It's been a doozie of a day, Jim," he said.

**Panel 5:** I went to work at the copy store today.

**Panel 6:** Hal, the manager, showed me how to run a big copy machine and got me started making 3,000 copies of something.

**Panel 7:** After about 3 minutes, the machine got jammed.

**Panel 8:** I went looking for Hal so he could show me how to fix it, then a customer told me her machine was jammed and asked me to fix it.

I worked at the copy store again today.

I was making 200 copies of somebody's resume.

I read a little bit of it while it was copying.

The person's career objective was "a public relations position allowing for skill enhancement and career growth."

Today as I was getting out of the shower, Mr. Peterson was looking inside the shower cautiously.

When I stepped out, I must have startled her because she ran away really fast.

At the copy store today I had to put finished copies into boxes.

The steady hum of all the copy machines makes the copy store sound like a factory sometimes.

Today Steve told me about a strange experience he had the other day.

He said he was in line at a fast food place when a guy started asking him to fight.

Steve said he was minding his own business, but the guy kept challenging him to a fight.

The guy eventually stopped bugging him, Steve said, but he still felt uncomfortable afterwards.

I made 9,000 copies of an advertising insert today.

When I got home I watched TV, ate a peanut butter and jelly sandwich and got really tired.

Today, Tony said he got a job interview with a big company.

"I gotta buy a suit — this is the big time, Jim," he told me.

We went out to get some ice cream.

I got a tutti-frutti cone and Tony said, "How can you get that? That's just about the worst flavor there is!"

Tony had me wish him luck on his big job interview today.

He was wearing his new suit.

I walked around outside for a while.

Then I came back home and watched TV.

I saw Tony today and asked him how it was going.

He said, "Don't ask," and walked into his room.

I saw him later and he told me his job interview yesterday was a disaster.

"The guy didn't even take me seriously," he said.

Today I went out for a walk.

I was cold at first, but got warmer after walking awhile.

I saw a fire hydrant that was painted all different colors.

I also saw a really old man who was hunched over quite a bit.

Today I was making some toast.

When it was finished, it popped out of the toaster hardly toasted at all.

So I put it back in the toaster.

When it popped up again, it was completely burnt.

Today Mr. Peterson woke me up.

meow
meow

I took her into the kitchen and put her by her food.

But she just walked away from it.

I noticed that our kitchen walls are kind of porous.

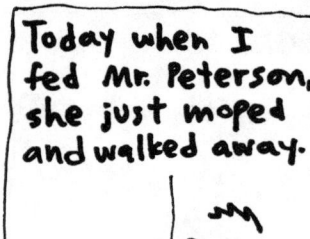

Today when I fed Mr. Peterson, she just moped and walked away.

She normally gets really excited when it's time to eat.

At the copy store today I had to make a whole bunch of copies of something.

They were on 8½"×14" paper.

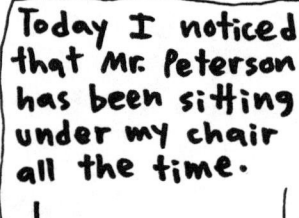

Today I noticed that Mr. Peterson has been sitting under my chair all the time.

She hardly ever sits under there.

I picked her up and she seemed really tired.

I felt her paws and her skin was dry and chapped.

I took Mr. Peterson to the veterinarian today.

The waiting room smelled like medicine, and cats and dogs were howling and making noises in the other rooms.

Mr. Peterson was trembling and trying to hide herself in my jacket.

When we went in to see the vet, I told her that Mr. Peterson was acting tired all the time and wasn't eating.

When I came home from the veterinarian yesterday, I ran into Tony.

Tony said, "Hey, how's it goin', cat?"

I told him Mr. Peterson just got some medication from the vet for having a virus.

Tony said his dog back home had heartworm or something and had to eat a huge pill every day.

Today when I fed Mr. Peterson I had to give her some medicine.

She eats it from an eye dropper. It's pink and smells like the veterinarian's office.

She doesn't like it and clenches up her face when I make her swallow it.

The vet said she should eat it for three weeks.

I went to the grocery store with Tony today and he showed me a test for buying frozen pizzas.

"Drop it from five feet up," he said. "If it bounces a little, it's a good one."

Then he said, "There's another test: can you throw it like a frisbee?"

He laughed, and when he saw that I wasn't laughing, he said, "You gotta get a sense of humor, Jim, I swear."

Today I was sitting around not doing much of anything.

Mr. Peterson was playing around, chasing and chewing a kleenex.

I took it away from her because I figured it was bad for her to be eating kleenex.

She did the same running around and playing, only without the kleenex.

Today Ruth and I went out for a walk.

She was telling me a story about something her mom did recently.

She was laughing out loud telling it.

But I didn't think it was all that funny.

Today I decided to clean the kitchen counter under my toaster.

I lifted the toaster up and there was a whole bunch of crumbs.

I dumped the crumbs out of the toaster. There were a lot of them.

Each time I thought I had dumped out all the crumbs, a few more would come out.

This morning Tony pounded on my door and said he forgot to buy food and needed something for breakfast.

"Come on, just anything, Jim," he said.

He looked like he was in a real hurry to get going.

I gave him a box of cereal I had and he said, "Aw, not this stuff!"

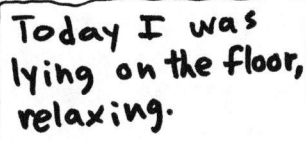

Today I was lying on the floor, relaxing.

I was looking at the ceiling, imagining what life would be like if the world was always upside-down.

Mr. Peterson came up to me and sniffed my face.

I could feel her tiny breaths, and her whiskers tickled my face.

Today I was looking up some place in the phone book that I had to call.

While I was flipping through the yellow pages I got sidetracked and just started looking at stuff.

Brake Service

Brass

Brass Fabricators

Brassieres

Breakfast Nooks

Brewery Equipment

Brick-Clay, Com and Face

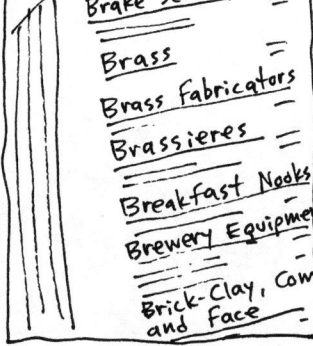

Contractors, General (cont'd)

Control Systems and Regulators

Convenience Stores

I worked at the copy store today.

Hal put me to work with someone reorganizing boxes of paper.

We started stacking boxes and she said, "You're new here."

I told her that I suppose you could say I'm new even though I've worked there almost a month.

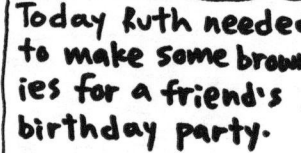

Today Ruth needed to make some brownies for a friend's birthday party.

I helped her make them.

(I mixed together the brownie mix with the eggs and water and stuff.)

Ruth told me all about her friend— she said she's known her since the third grade.

At the copy store today I was just cleaning up stuff around the floor.

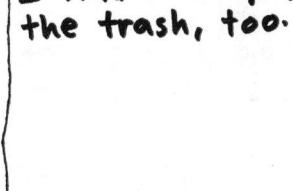

I had to empty the trash, too.

It was really sunny outside, and with all the windows in the copy store, it was really bright in there.

I looked at Hal, who was helping a customer. The sun was shining onto the back of his head and his ear looked bright orange.

Today at the copy store one of the people I work with, Joel, said he was going to San Francisco.

I told him my mom just went to San Francisco for a piano-teachers convention.

He didn't seem too interested.

After I said it I realized it wasn't a very interesting thing to say.

Ruth wanted to go bowling with me and Steve, so we went last night.

It was a lot of fun, even though we weren't any good.

The funniest thing that happened was when Steve let go of his ball wrong.

It rolled straight into the gutter without even touching the lane.

This morning Tony asked me to come over and listen to what happened to him last night.

It was complicated, but centered around his almost getting arrested in front of a bar.

"I met this awesome girl, too—damn, I wish I'd got her name!" he said.

His voice was low and gravelly because of it being so early in the morning.

Today Tony was playing his new tape when it started to slow down.

It slowed down more, then suddenly stopped.

He took it out of the tape-player and it was completely unraveled and crumpled.

"Oh, dammit!" he said. "Dammit, dammit, dammit!"

Today Tony was playing another tape and it suddenly slowed to a stop.

"I've had it," he said. "Do you know how many tapes I've lost to this thing?"

He grabbed the machine and smashed it against the wall, the table, and the floor.

Little knobs and stuff shot across the room and the machine got pretty badly bent up.

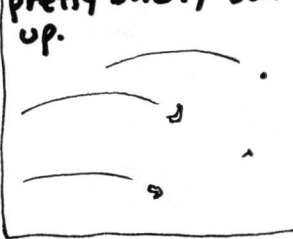

Julie is one of the people I work with at the copy store.

Today she set the controls for some copies I had to make, and she did it a lot faster than I can.

Hal, the manager, came up to us and said, "As soon as you two are finished here, I've got another job for you."

We both guessed that the job was to make copies on another machine.

I worked at the copy store today.

I had to get up really early to work the morning shift.

I was tired, and just stared into space. I didn't pay attention to what I was doing.

If I relaxed enough, and blocked out all my senses, I could almost sleep standing up.

"Everybody in the whole world has a CD-player except me," Tony said today.

He listed some of the people he knew who had CD-players

He said he wanted to buy one this friday, at a place that's having a sale.

"What the hell is this cat's problem?" he said.

I went with Tony today to a place where he was going to buy a CD-player.

As we were walking into the store, he said, "The salespeople in these places can be real animals."

He said they practically assault you and sell you things you don't want.

We stood near the CD-players and waited for a salesperson, but nobody came for a long time.

Today I started work at the copy store at 6pm

As I got there, Hal, Joel and Julie were just leaving.

They looked like they were glad to be done working and going out to have fun.

Brian and I were the only ones working.

(Brian likes to play the radio when he works.)

Today I saw Tony coming home.

He was carrying a little plastic bag.

He didn't say anything as he walked past me. He just jiggled the bag and smiled.

I could see that it had a CD in it.

Today I worked the evening shift with Brian at the copy store.

Hardly anybody came in.

Brian and I didn't have much work to do.

He asked me if I'd mind if he turned the radio up louder and I said not really.

It was really cold today so I wore a hat.

When I took it off I could feel that part of my hair was sticking up.

At night I was just lying in bed.

I touched my head and found that my hair was still sticking up in that spot.

Today I was throwing around a little ball for Mr. Peterson.

I was trying to throw it right to her so she'd catch it.

But she would bat it away instead.

Also today I watched The Flash on TV and even though Steve doesn't like the show, I thought it was okay.

Today I was walking outside for a while.

It was snowing.

I saw some people playing and throwing snowballs at each other.

(I was on the other side of the street, so I didn't get hit with any snowballs.)

I went to the store today to buy some food.

While I was waiting in line I looked at the tabloids.

There was a story about a werewolf baby that was pretty funny.

After a while a woman standing in front of me said, "This express lane isn't very expressive, is it?"

I ate lunch with Ruth today.

She was telling me what her ten favorite popular songs were.

(She was trying to list them in order, one through ten.)

When she finished, she thought maybe she should switch songs nine and ten around.

I walked by somebody on the sidewalk today.

He was a big guy who stood there and smiled as I walked past him.

"It's a miracle," he said, "Life is a miracle!"

I didn't respond to him and kept walking, but I kept hearing him in my head over and over.

I got up early for work today.

I fed Mr. Peterson. She was really hungry, as always.

At the copy store I made 200 copies of some kind of office report.

I pictured Mr. Peterson eating, bobbing her head like she does.

At the copy store today a customer wanted me to make a copy for her.

So I did.

She handed me a dollar bill that had a ripped corner.

She asked if we could accept it and I said I guess we could.

Mr. Peterson ran out the door again when I came home today.

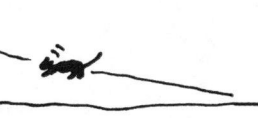
I let her stay in the hall for a while, and she seemed very interested in exploring.

Then, down the hall, somebody closed a door and the noise startled her.

She ran inside and stayed there

Today I was walking outside.

While I was walking I saw someone walking toward me.

Suddenly he turned around and started walking in the opposite direction.

I guess he must have forgotten something.

Today at the copy store Hal, the manager, was working along with everybody else.

He likes to laugh and kid around a lot.

But whenever he does, he ends it by saying, "Alright, enough monkeying around, let's get back to work."

He doesn't say it in those exact words every time, but generally that's what he does.

I sat in bed this morning before I got up and pictured myself as infinitely big one second, then as small as a pea the next. This happened over and over, like a strobe light, for about 20 seconds.

I visited Ruth today.

when I came to her apartment she apologized for it being such a mess.

But it looked perfectly clean and tidy to me.

I worked at the copy store today.

I overheard Hal talking to someone about Brian being "on thin ice."

I guessed that Hal thought Brian was doing a bad job, even though I'd never noticed.

I worked with Brian that night and kept thinking about what Hal said.

Today I decided to vacuum my floor.

Mr. Peterson hid under the table and watched the vacuum cleaner intently.

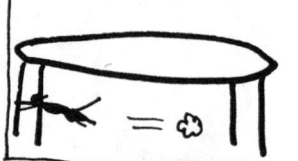
When I headed toward her, she got scared and ran away.

I worked at the copy store with Brian last night.

I noticed he was making some two-sided copies with one side upside-down.

I pointed it out to him and he said, "Oops," then chuckled.

I wondered if I would have noticed his mistake if I hadn't heard Hal talking about Brian doing a bad job.

| | | | |
|---|---|---|---|
| Mr. Peterson was taking a nap on the floor today. | She was sleeping in a spot where the sun was shining through the window. | She stretched herself out and then turned up on her back. | Then suddenly she looked at me and said, "Pleep!" |
|  |  |  |  |
| Today Steve came over and said he was getting rid of all his Spider Man comic books. | He asked if I wanted them and I said no. | I asked him why he was getting rid of them. | And he said he just couldn't think of any reason to have them. |
|  |  |  |  |

Today I was walking home from work at night.

I looked up at the sky while I walked.

I realized it'd been a long time since I just looked at the sky.

I thought maybe I've been cooped up too much lately.

I had to get up early today to go work at the copy store.

I really didn't feel like getting up at all.

But I did anyway because I had to.

After I was up for a while I wasn't that tired anymore.

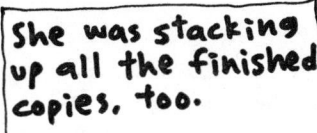
Today at the copy store Julie was making copies.

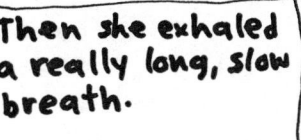
She was stacking up all the finished copies, too.

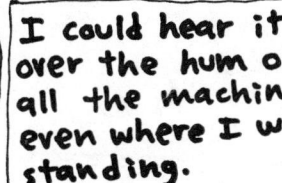
Then she exhaled a really long, slow breath.

I could hear it over the hum of all the machines even where I was standing.

I ran into the guy from down the hall today.

I was walking in and passed him by the door.

"How's the weather out there today?" he said.

I told him it was okay.

**Today** Tony, Steve and I went to a movie.

Tony got some milk duds and a Pepsi and said. "Nature's perfect food!"

Steve went to the rest rooms and Tony said, "What's he doing? The movie's gunna start any second."

Steve came back right when the movie started.

Today I went to visit Ruth.

On top of her TV I noticed some clay casts of teeth.

She's a dental assistant, so I thought they were things she got from her job.

But she said they were casts of her own teeth, "when I was 5, 12 and 17 years old," she said.

I worked at the copy store almost eight hours today.

When I got home I was really tired.

I moved the TV next to my bed so I could lie down, relax, and watch whatever was on.

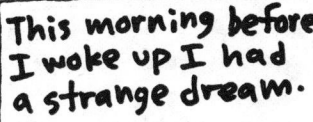

This morning before I woke up I had a strange dream.

I was in a big building full of people that was having a really loud fire alarm.

The alarm sounded a lot like Mr. Peterson meowing.

Then I realized it was just a dream and that Mr. Peterson was probably meowing right next to my ear.

Today Ruth and I went over to see Steve.

He was eating an apple when we came in.

"To what do I owe the pleasure of your company?" he asked.

We said we just stopped by—no particular reason.

Today Brian said his friend was in a band and was performing at a bar that night.

He said, "It should be a good show—I'm excited about it."

I was making some copies that came out with little black splotches on them.

I wiped off the glass and that took care of the problem.

I was sitting around today feeling pretty bored.

Mr. Peterson walked by me a couple times, meowing to herself.

Then she hopped up on the chair and sat in my lap, but didn't sleep.

I guess she was feeling bored today too.

Today at the copy store things were really slow.

Brian asked me if I'd mind if he smoked, and I said not really.

Then someone came in to make some self-service copies and asked Brian if he'd mind putting out his cigarette.

Brian said, "Hey, sure, man. No problem. That's cool," and put it out.

**Panel 1:** At the copy store today Brian and I were preparing a bunch of copies for somebody.

**Panel 2:** Brian suddenly said, "I don't feel like doing this," and went over by the counter.

**Panel 3:** I asked him why he doesn't seem to like working here very much.

**Panel 4:** He said, "It's not _my_ copy store—I can only care so much."

**Panel 5:** I came home today around 6 p.m.

**Panel 6:** when I opened the door, Mr. Peterson shot outside really fast.

**Panel 7:** I went to get her and she cowered away from me like she was afraid for her life.

**Panel 8:** Once I got her back inside, she sat by the door and meowed.

meow  meow

Ruth came over to visit today.

She picked up Mr. Peterson and said, "Hello there!"

Mr. Peterson stared at Ruth with a surprised, wide-eyed look on her face.

Ruth stared back at Mr. Peterson with the same wide-eyed look.

Today I walked by the bookstore where I used to work.

I started remembering all the times I spent there.

I didn't really like working there back then, but for some reason I had nice memories of it.

**Panel 1:** I sat around and watched TV today.

**Panel 2:** After a while I got bored with the TV so I turned it off.

**Panel 3:** While I sat there, I started to feel like I was floating.

**Panel 5:** I sat around and watched TV for a while today.

**Panel 6:** I watched Unsolved Mysteries and they had a story about a UFO landing in Pennsylvania.

**Panel 7:** They made it sound like it could have actually happened.

**Panel 8:** I thought it was a pretty good show.

Today Tony came by and said, "Hey, Jim, you're gonna love this..."

He had a little rubber puppet thing that was just a face that contorted when he moved his fingers.

Tony growled when the face looked angry, hollered when the face's mouth was wide open, and had fun making silly faces with it.

"Isn't this just the greatest thing?" he said.

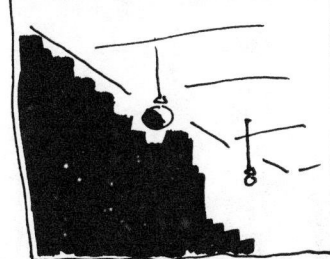
When I came home today I noticed the light by my door was burned out.

I had a hard time trying to find my key because it was so dark.

I thought I should call the landlord about it.

But I didn't feel like doing it right then.

When I came home today I had to try to find my keys in the dark hallway.

I came in and saw Mr. Peterson sitting by the door.

I sat there and petted her for a while.

Today Tony told me about a dream he had last night.

"It was wild, Jim, you wouldn't have believed it," he said.

He said he had a race car that could take him anywhere in the world in 2 seconds.

"But the weird thing is," he said, "I only went to my Aunt Helen's house and a meat-packing plant."

I worked at the copy store today and a lot of people were coming in.

I made tons of copies and worked the cash register, too.

Once I noticed Ruth walking by outside.

She didn't see me, and I was too busy to stop and talk or anything anyway.

As I was coming home today I saw the guy from down the hall.

He was walking more slowly than usual.

He walked by me without saying anything.

I tried to find my door key in the dark hall.

(I still haven't called the landlord about the burned-out light.)

| | | | |
|---|---|---|---|
| I worked at the copy store today. | I was there earlier than I usually am. | Hal, the manager, Julie, and Joel were all there. | Things weren't as laid back as when just Brian and I are working the evening shift. |
|  |  |  |  |
| Today Tony was walking home with me. | We got to my door and I couldn't find my key right away because the hall light is burned out. | "You should call the landlord about that," Tony said. | When we got inside, Tony told me he has a good chance of working at an ad agency. |
|  |  |  |  |

 Today I was just sitting around.

 Then Tony came by.

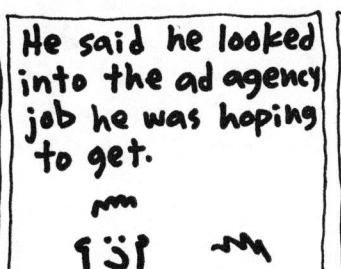 He said he looked into the ad agency job he was hoping to get.

 "All they want is some stooge to sit in the xerox room all day and make copies!" he said.

 Tony was talking today about the ad agency job he was trying to get.

 He said he couldn't believe the job was in the xerox room and not in the sales or creative dept.

 "I have a college education for Pete's sake!" he said. "In economics!"

 "I know all about money and ads and stuff."

Today I got up a little late.

The clock-radio alarm went off about a half hour before I got up.

Somehow I slept through it and didn't even hear it.

I fed Mr. Peterson and she ate up her food like crazy.

Today I was bored and was just sitting up on my big chair.

I started to rock the chair back and forth.

I felt like I was going to fall over any minute.

when I eventually did, it didn't hurt or anything. It was even kind of fun.

I worked at the copy store today.

But I didn't really feel like I was there.

My body did all the walking around and making copies.

But my mind was somewhere else.

I went to the pet store today to get more food for Mr. Peterson.

They had some new kittens there, so I looked at them for a while.

They were asleep, and didn't move much when I touched them.

I couldn't believe how small they were.

I got up and sat around this morning.

Then I went to the copy store and worked from noon to 5:30.

Then I came home and watched TV for a while.

When the day was over, it struck me how unremarkable a day it had been.

This morning I was lying in bed trying to sleep.

But Mr. Peterson was walking around meowing.

Once, she hopped up right in front of me and looked at me.

I asked her what the heck she was meowing about and she just meowed again.

As I was coming home today I noticed a repairman in the hall.

He was replacing the light bulb by my door.

I kept forgetting to call the landlord about it.

I guess they found out about it from somebody else.

Today I went to Tony's apartment and he was watching TV.

He was flipping between the channels with his remote control.

He was flipping through channels faster and faster.

Finally he just held down the channel-changing button—the channels flipped by so fast the screen was just a blur.

Today I was making copies of a story somebody wrote.

I thought it might be fun to read while I copied it.

But I was copying it too fast, so I couldn't have kept up with it even if I'd wanted to.

So I just stood there and stared off into space.

Today at the copy store one of the copy machines broke down.

Hal took a look at it and said he knew what the problem was.

He stuck a pen in there and poked it around.

Everybody stood around and watched him even though it wasn't very interesting.

steve came by today.

"How's it goin', Mr. P," he said to Mr. Peterson.

She completely ignored him and walked right by.

"Hey, Jim, guess what I did," he said, and then he told me he signed up for a sailboating class.

I saw the guy from down the hall today.

He passed by me and said, "How are you today," in a really loud voice.

I said I was fine.

"Hard not to be on a day like today, eh?"

(It was a nice and sunny day today.)

Today I walked by a fast food restaurant.

It had a big sign in the window that said "Now Hiring."

DIKKERS

But the window frame blocked part of the sign so it looked like "Now Firing."

NOW FIRING

I thought that was kind of funny.

Today I started thinking about what it would be like if I worked at the copy store my whole life.

I'd be the manager and I'd know everything about the store.

I don't know why I was thinking about it.

DIKKERS

It was kind of depressing.

Today when I came to work Brian wasn't there.

I asked where he was and somebody said, "He quit."

"He's lucky he quit when he did," Hal said, "'cause he was on his last leg anyway."

It struck me what a tough, cutthroat place the copy store really is.

Today at the copy store Julie and I were the only ones working.

I was on the cash register and Julie was making copies.

I asked if she'd mind switching jobs for a while and she said, "oh, great."

I couldn't tell if she was being serious or completely sarcastic.

**Panel 1:** I was outside walking around today.

**Panel 2:** I noticed a delivery truck or something parked on the street.

**Panel 3:** I looked up close at one of the tires.

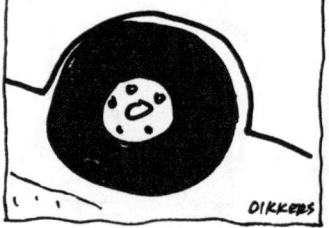

**Panel 4:** It had a lot of ridges, and little things that looked like tiny rubber whiskers sticking out of it.

**Panel 5:** I hung around with Ruth today.

**Panel 6:** We took a bus to a mall.

**Panel 7:** (She likes to go to malls to look at stuff.)

**Panel 8:** When we were in the mall she said, "I bet they have a store for everything here."

Today I worked at the copy store all day.

I came home and was so tired I just fell right onto my bed and fell asleep.

I woke up at 2 a.m. and was wide awake.

There was nothing else to do, so I played with Mr. Peterson till dawn.

When I woke up today I was lying on the floor with Mr. Peterson snuggled into my neck.

I looked at the clock and saw that it was noon.

I was supposed to be at work at 9 a.m., so I hurried to the copy store.

When I got there Hal said, "Jim—we all thought you were dead."

I was glad that he didn't seem to care that I was so late.

This morning at the copy store a lot of people were working.

I was kind of tired, and we were disorganized and bumping into each other.

Hal came up from the back room and clapped his hands and said. "Let's go, gang— look alive!"

I suddenly felt even more tired than I did before.

Today I sat on a bench and ate an apple.

It was a nice sunny day and a lot of people were outside.

Someone with a little girl walked by me and the girl was looking at me.

Then she smiled and tried to hide behind her mom so I couldn't see her.

Today I was getting something to drink from a pop machine with Tony.

I put my money in and the can came right out.

Tony put his coins in, pushed the knob, and nothing happened. "Oh, no!" he said.

Then, after a couple seconds, the can came tumbling down. "Whew!" Tony said.

I decided to go out and visit my mom for a while.

"Nice of you to drop by once every eon or so," she said.

She asked how everything was going and I said everything was going fine.

Her cookie jar was full of cream-filled oatmeal cookies.

Today my mom showed me a bunch of pictures from her trip to San Francisco.

She told me how much fun she had and how nice the city was.

She had a new story to tell for each picture.

After that I took a nap.

Last night I slept in my mom's guest room.

It's kept clean and perfectly neat when no one's in it.

I felt like I was trashing it just by being there.

When I got up today my mom was out doing something.

(she left a note.)

| | | | |
|---|---|---|---|
| I went over to my dad's house today.  | "Well, hello there," my dad said.  | He took me behind his house to show me a new thing he just bought that he said he was really excited about.  | It was a big motorcycle.  |
| I came back home today after visiting my parents.  | Ruth was in my apartment.  (She took care of Mr. Peterson while I was gone.) | She hugged Mr. Peterson and said, "She's been such a good kitty."  | Then Mr. Peterson jumped out of her arms and ran away and hid.  |